# futurus integer...

## A list of poems

Celestial Siren

author-HOUSE®

*AuthorHouse™*
*1663 Liberty Drive*
*Bloomington, IN 47403*
*www.authorhouse.com*
*Phone: 1-800-839-8640*

*First published by AuthorHouse     5/12/2010*

*ISBN: 978-1-4490-8949-8 (sc)*

*Printed in the United States of America*
*Bloomington, Indiana*

*This book is printed on acid-free paper.*

I would like to thank all the people who inspired my poems, they may not know who they are... I may not even know who all of them are. Never the less they made me a little less useless and I'd like to thank them for that. A special thanks goes out also, and especially to the one who inspires my very being in every way imaginable, God. He is the real author behind these poems.

# Contents

# DARK POEMS

"For scarcely for a righteous man would one die, yet peradventure for a good man some would even dare to die." (Romans 5:7)

# Like you're Immortal

In a town, unlike your own,
A secret place, an unsafe zone,
A place of evil, beyond all doubt,
Where cries are dulled, amidst a drought,
A drought of darkness, of fevered greed,
There every desire becomes a need,
A night closes in, even blacker than before,
Your sight is then blinded, but there's more,
For lack of light, yet is there a glow,
Of creatures vile, a beastly foe,
With lust for blood, it prowls alone,
Agile like a child, yet with strength no man has known,
Skin like chalk, eyes like a hawk, its beauty a flame,
A dangerous predator, you need not know its name,
For madness is, and was, and has become,
A brave man's hidden desire, to alas be succumb,
For though adventure is lush and sweet,
Without a purpose, you're destined for defeat.

# Sweet Revenge

Darkness, a chilling bliss,
An iridescent flow of light to calm, a terror beyond imagination,
A light in the dark, like a cold drink to the parched throat,
The flow of passion moving through an iron wall,
A key with no lock, like a shepherd with no flock,
A wild mist swirls above, a gaping hole void of love,
Eyes like fire, lips like ice; blood like lava, a roll of dice,
Fortune spins, fate falls short, destiny calls, kismet claims,
Anger comes, when patience slips,
Retribution is honey to my lips.

# Asmodeus

When the blood turns black,
O that's when they'll attack,
When the sunlight fails,
All earths' beauty pales,
I see a light above,
A sickly green void of love,
For in my madness, all joy is mellowed,
Whilst under such torment, the darkness I followed,
Away from all mirth, my insides did stir,
A sadistic chaos, within me, became my lure,
For now while the world is young and naïve,
Their minds will be mine to twist and deceive.

# The Birth of Sadism

Moonlight pale, as night grows grim,
A star shines bright; no notice is paid him,
For in the west, darkness rises,
A flame of white, full of surprises,
For in its glow, a life is stolen,
A once strong soul, alas has fallen,
Yet dead, he is not for nature is twisted,
His once wholesome morals, all at once are misted,
The beast, his slayer, hath taken his humanity,
Damned his soul, to quench his vanity,
A life of beauty, void of pain,
To kill without mercy, for one's own gain.

# Inner Pestilence

The sun was out, its beauty shone iridescently along the edges of my skin,
its glory radiated in rays across my face, but fell away without so much as a smile to lighten it's shimmering countenance, the sun's glow was no more then skin deep, for in the depths of my soul a black abyss was rapidly forming, taking every joy and merriment within me, with which it forms its jagged edges. I felt torn, but physically like something was tearing apart my insides, my love, my laughter, my every waking desire, leaving doubt and despair in its place. As light evaporates, and darkness consumes, it reminds me that I'm alone; when the hole is finally gaping I will dwindle. My mind, my emotions, my spirit, my everything, will be caught up in my masochistic destitution. To which I'm bound. I look for a light amidst the darkness, but there is none, yet there isn't really any darkness. Just an illusion, a desire for it instead of what it truly is. It's as though the life has been strangled from me, and I am no longer among the living.
I move slowly through a sea of faces, but see nothing. Its as though I don't exist, I walk around void of my body, in a world that is not my own, among people who are nothing like me, they neither see, nor sense me. I am like Iocaine powder drifting along suffocating the life out of all I touch. but I'm not completely empty, no, I'm over flowing with merciless tormentors, stabbing at my insides, choking whatever life still remains hid within me.
A knife is in their hand, it stabs relentlessly until the tormentor grows angry
And finally declares that, 'it's dead!' Everything within is dead. There is no more to harm, for its broken beyond repair." It leaves me then wallowing in a pool of sorrow and remorse for what I lost. The sadness dies, for I no longer remember what I lost. It's as if it was never there in the first place, like there never was anything,
I was a stranger to nothing, yet nothing to a stranger.
I no longer care.
I am drained of self pity.
I pity nothing, I desire nothing.
I sit now with now with no memory of what I really am.
And am nothing that will ever be found in ones memory.

# Miser's Madness

Avaricious, it is said of he,
Who claims that mirth demands a fee,
For once way-laid in gluttony,
Wealth is now ones agony,
Amidst the sorrowful pain you plea,
To "send forth mirth", now deprived of thee,
Now you mourn whilst high and lusty,
For like your gold, all joy grows dusty.

# Moral Decay

When words fall short, and daylight dies,
All mouths fall silent, whilst moonlight cries,
A shadow rules, when stars grow dim,
The air will chill, as all turns grim,
Mortal youth alas is weak,
Their voices dry, though they wish to speak,
For that right was stolen, by darkness itself,
They wish to fight, yet lack the strength,
The night grows long, and hope is lost,
The air is cold, and the ground begins to frost,
The sun then returns, with rays of poison,
That boils the blood, and eats at their skin,
All at once, the night becomes bliss,
Sickly sweet, with a honey-like kiss,
They linger long, their words still few,
The morning comes, they flee on cue,
For night is their pleasure, a passion with dread,
They rejoice in her coming, for life as they know it is dead.

# A Mundane Truth

The human heart is unstable, a bigots life a fable,
The mortal mind is twisted, easily swayed by the gifted,
Alas all truth is gone, enticed in lust, you turn to wrong,
When laws give way, the wicked doth play,
A superfluity of naughtiness, a chaos of lawlessness,
Your cities will flourish, while life dost perish,
An escape they now seek, yet their cries are far from meek,
They lay as though slain, being bitter, wanton, and spiteful with pain,
But still they are distraught, and peace shall grace them not,
Though gentle is a rippling brook, a devilish soul shall alas be forsook.

# The Cost of Free Will

A blackened heart, awakes beneath,
With eyes like ice, he bars his teeth,
A gentle growl escapes his lips,
And fury, menacing, he now equips,
He wants his life back, the one that faded,
The one that reins, is way past jaded,
He cannot hold his own emotion,
For it no longer, to him, holds devotion,
It has no master for his thoughts are ill,
For it has one desire, an urge to kill,
To swallow the infectious tears that takes a corrosive toll,
To grind the venomous humanity that cripples his very soul,
For love is a surrender of all that is yourself,
And his self could not allow such a hazard to his health,
Barred away the victim lays a slave to the unknown,
For his emotions would not do this, he knows them, they are his own,
He scowls, he frets, and he bites at his wrists,
Which he alas recalls had once bore a kiss,
The memory however vague in truth,
Had brought a vision of his youth,
He saw at once the sun so pure,
For its shimmer had only increased her lure,
She was not vile, as he had let himself believe,
She radiated a joy, to which he alone she did bequeath,
How could it be that she held such power?
He had been released; yet his thoughts were sour,
Did he want to go would he now surrender?
If she had faded would he dare avenge her?
The thought brought forth a glimpse of peace,
But he knew right then the pain would never cease,
His wrestling thoughts were strong yet sincere,
For love pure, and simple had slaughtered his fear.

# Good riddance

Your words had never gone down smoothly, which is why I should have known,
That your childish ways are from cute, I thought that you had grown,
Your lies washed over me, as a salt sea wave,
They left a bad taste, as I suffered in my grave,
You put me there, though you'd hardly admit it,
I would've asked more questions, but I knew you'd forbid it,
You would not stop with your reign of terror,
And I knowingly aided you, my aren't you clever,
You knew me well, and you found my weakness,
So I failed to see through your studied deepness,
You made me want it, and I knew I did,
So young and naïve, that I did as you bid,
You told me tales, and fantasies like they were truth,
When I came up for air, I stood in awe of your great spoof,
I'll have you know your plot did not fail,
But I'm afraid when I leave; the wind will leave your sail,
I know you're strong; I made you that way,
But now that I'm gone, I'm afraid you're easy prey,
I'm not afraid, in fact, I'm glad,
For you held me back, you were nothing but a passing fad.

# A Wayward Fall

I once had faith, I once was strong,
But now the whole idea of it, just seems so wrong,
I want to jump, but the cliff is so steep,
I want to accept, but don't make a peep,
My thoughts are loose and never stable,
I wish to say no, but never am able,
The idea alone, makes my stomach queasy,
This thing may be rare, but far too cheesy,
I say my answer, though it wouldn't be right,
to begin when I know it will end in a fight.

# A Rude Awakening

It's quiet in my prison, no light dost grace my cell,
The darkness serves as my blanket; some might call it hell,
Me, I call it home, for these walls have fathered my tears,
It's strange; I can't see my reflection, since this room is filled with mirrors,
Black on black, yet I can see the seam,
A green glow rises I feel I'm in a dream,
Never once was there color permitted,
Yet this lonely glow had alas been admitted,
I glare at the glow, hoping it might retreat,
Yet am met with my reflection, all at once I claim defeat,
The face that stares back is nothing short a nightmare,
The ghoulish features, made livid by unruly hair,
I cringe in fear and hide my face, praying it leave me be,
I cry aloud and beat on the glass; I want alas to be free,
I could endure the darkness and liked to be lonesome,
But I could no longer stand it when I saw what I'd become,
I wasn't just a hermit, I was in truth, a picture of death,
When I beheld my visage, I completely lost my breath.

# Arachno-cat

Sleep ails me but, does not overcome me, I will not let it,
For my window is always opened and a candle always lit,
You see if I sleep, then I will dream,
A dream that relays, a tormenting theme,
For in my dream an evil comes to terrify me alone,
My imagination, alive, awakes fears I had never known,
Darkness stirs in a place filled with beauty,
This darkness intends to keep me from my duty,
Its face so sweet, yet its body is morbid,
The image remains, its visage I'll never be rid,
My only chance is to face this fear,
And stand my ground, when it starts to sneer,
For if I keep it near and never let it go,
The fear will then diminish, since it has no room to grow.

# Dream catcher

When darkness falls, it is then the nightmares come,
When night grows grim it is then I wish to run,
For what dost follow is oh so terrible,
I delve beneath my covers and claim it's unbelievable,
I want to cry, I want to scream,
But this thing that comes is more than it dost seem,
I pray a prayer and shut my eyes, hoping it will be gone,
I have this fear, that while I sleep, everything can go wrong,
I try to wake, but I'm too far spent,
I try to resist, but this creature won't relent,
He doesn't exist "he's just my imagination" I cry,
The creature recoils and slowly saunters by,
I feel his touch, but it melts away,
The dream has dissolved, for now anyway.

# Dark Devastation

Night time shortens a day of spite,
It silence the sun in a display of might,
Its desire is nameless but its will is done,
It lifts its arms and blocks out the sun,
I hide within its darkened street,
Along this road, not a soul will I meet,
Why do I cry, when I get my way?
I hide from light, till it alas turned gray,
My tears came fast, so no one would see,
That thing within that torments me,
My crying will stop, when I succumb to sleep,
Yet I'm wide awake, for my hurt is deep,
Sometimes I wish someone would spy,
Someone I could love, would see me cry,
I don't know why I have this desire,
To love what I hate, would make me a liar,
The sky grows darker and my tears turn to rain,
This blessed shower dost mask my pain,
I bathe in its essence, till I'm totally drenched,
I refuse to shiver, for my jaw is clenched,
"This feels amazing," the words are true,
I feel refreshed, all clean and new,
I know I must leave, but the mud dost smile,
A moment of joy, makes my body agile,
A sudden leap, bids my worries adieu,
Yet I fear when they return, it'll feel as if they grew.

# A Quelled Heart

A heart in chains, locked away from all commotion,
Hidden from harm, this heart requires no devotion,
It needs a home, for it rests in a cell,
Its needs are fruitless, for it dwells in hell,
This torment is its own design,
So that the world will think it's fine,
Keeping busy, keeps the emotions away,
An empty agenda, has a price to pay,
How can it survive, wrapped up in its chains?
It thinks its restraints, will mask its pains,
It thinks, it feels, it shows no feeling,
Its only response, is that it's dealing,
It wants to be free, it has a purpose,
Its owner is stubborn, they will not discuss,
They know they'll lose, the heart is stronger,
It will take a stand, when it can't take it any longer,
It will find, the key, or bloody break the lock,
If it melted the chains, it wouldn't be a shock,
My heart has the power, it will know when its time,
It will burst from its chains and let its love shine.

# Life's Lie

Renewed life flows slowly over a blood drained heart,
You wait in silence as it all falls apart,
Light circulates through a forest in solitude,
With the world far beneath you, you sense a new altitude,
A wind takes root to the pattern of your limbs,
It's hard to have control as life around you swims,
Are you really standing or has nature taken control,
Do your feet move in accordance with your will to stroll?
You can't be alive; your heart beat has slowed,
Water saturates, where blood once flowed,
You feel so weak, for your strength is not your own,
Your display of might is proof that you're not alone,
Control is not a luxury that you could ever merit,
Could it be that this handicap is something you inherit?
Even when you thought each step you took was planned,
You had always felt this presence struggling to take command,
Alas you greatest desire is to surrender and cry,
These desires are eluded for your tear ducts have run dry,
You can sense the hurt, for the sting is fatally sharp,
This torment resounds, like the plucking of a harp,
A cry is uttered, but your lips don't move,
A desire is muttered; you have everything to prove,
You have no will, not a single action thought out,
Your lips speak words you know nothing about,
The language is foreign but the words emanate beauty,
You seek their meaning; you feel it is your duty,
To know these words could be the essence of fulfillment,
The meaning therewith would bring with it all contentment,
You're speaking nonsense, yet it all makes sense,
These simple seductions dost embody your essence,
A wonder is known, but is eschewed from your vision,
An end is at hand, it is your own decision,
Wonder lies in all things that retain life,
It issues forth peace, whilst beset in strife,

# BEAUTY POEMS

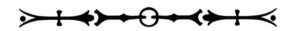

# Dauntless Serenity

Blessed with beauty, she sheaths herself in light,
Innocence masks, what unveils her might,
A beautiful soldier, a deadly rose,
She grows from rain, a garden she sows,
A simple problem, a mystery without magnitude,
How can someone so sweet, possess so much attitude?
From a well of springs she makes herself known,
She has no wings, but you could swear she's flown,
Your stomach is sick yet all is well,
Secrets take form, yet none can tell,
She wants a name, but to her, none is given,
Nothings seems to suit a soul this driven,
She wanders in darkness, yet somehow she glows,
Her perfect flesh, reflects rainbows,
Her words are song, a blessing imparted,
The tune fills your mind, while her lips are parted,
Her skin is golden, like the sand of the desert,
She is so gentle, yet she brings great hurt,
It's not her fault, it's part of her guise,
For this flower can claim your heart with her eyes.

# A golden night

Bitterness, frost, a chilling December,
Rage and furry, how it seeks to dismember,
It flares, it spits, an act of disgust,
Discomfort it knows, a fear of trust,
For when it moves, your insides will shutter,
Your eyes are enraptured, while your lips do mutter,
You can taste the air, foreign yet familiar,
You seem changed, different, but similar,
You want to laugh, you want to scream,
But your lips are silent, your not what you seem,
It comes once more, your caught off guard,
You look to turn, for your ego is marred,
You know your place, there never was a doubt,
How can one be betrayed, by someone so devote.

# Lightness of Mind

The sun is out, he wants to play,
He tickles my cheek, as he colors the day,
My hair, golden, as it reflects the suns color,
This flawless companion is like none other,
He's always there when I'm feeling down,
Amidst his rays, I continually drown,
My flesh is speckled, as a result of his radiance,
The cheer he spreads, is nothing short of immense,
I wonder I whisper, a sun-kissed secret,
I ask him once, for he'd never forget,
He has this song, that he plays for my amusement,
It makes me laugh and of my questions I repent,
I was not meant to know his secrets,
For the answers are followed with many regrets,
He knows I'm young so he'll play the toy,
For he takes great pleasure in my joy,
I wander wordless as his rays kiss my eyes,
And yearn alas to dwell amidst his skies.

# At One with Nature

Tired of the wandering mountains, that flash across the horizon,
You look to sleep, but feel an adrenaline rising,
A mesh of Ash trees, now spirit on by,
You're moving so fast, you feel as though you can fly,
A clever moon now flushes with a glint of amber,
It calls you home with its brazen lure,
You check your senses, as a smile tickles your stiffened cheek,
You feel so alive, you're unable to speak,
A forest awakes, as the sun begins to set,
The endless field's hunger, will then be met,
A glow then bursts forth, with flames of red,
The night now awakens, thinking the sun is dead,
An aura then sweeps over the land, like a flood,
A compelling emotion, now heats my blood,
At this rate I shall never sleep,
While the wiles of nature, possess my feet.

# The Color of Nature

Crimson life, a clear blue shadow,
Awakens in an evergreen meadow,
The sky is pallid, streaked with jade,
Lilac ice, now weeps, as it's unmade,
A golden sun, lit by sapphire seas,
As amber leaves, fall from emerald trees,
A mist gleams silver, amidst the fun,
And races at once, to eclipse a topaz sun,
It does not fight back, but dulls till sage,
From aqua it dost return, in an amethyst rage,
Fierce is its return, for the sky is red,
And that playful gray mist, for now, is dead.

# Seasons

A frigid wind is in the air,
It numbs your toes and tousles your hair,
It assaults the sun, whilst you bathe in its glow,
A deadly poisoned shadow all at once is your foe,
Frozen rage hath scathed your skin,
A chill down your spine, rises from deep within,
A sickly sadist, he's claimed in truth,
His chilling torment, no longer a spoof,
For his methods, raw, hath claimed the breeze,
The now weak sun, can't purge his disease,
When snow shimmer's white, the sun grows strong,
Musters its rays in the form of a throng,
Then releases his power in beams of light,
Warming the soil and giving the trees delight,
Licks at the ice, with his tongue of fire,
Waking the waters, to suffice its earth's desire,
For now while the world is at war with itself,
We can experience seasons, and all their stealth,

# In the Light

The gold sun shines on all that is gay,
Chasing the shadows, and coloring the gray,
I want this joy to last forever,
To crush the darkness, and make things better,
The sun is my friend, my light, my brother,
I want him always, to leave me never,
His warmth dries my tears,
While his glow hides my fears,
If I were to die, I'd take him with me,
Just to tag along, and help me see,
For without him near, I am already dead,
His absence fills my mind with dread,
So linger now, my beloved sun,
Shed your rays, for the day has barely begun.

# Mana Malaise

Pallid in circumference, and hair a translucent violet,
When this foe strikes, her methods are far from violent,
Your vision is clouded, when beholding her beauty,
Her pearl eyes penetrate, while a touch completes her duty,
She takes as she pleases, but she is no thief,
For in your weakness, your will you will bequeath,
Your will is then hers, to wield as she desires,
But without a motive, her plot lacks, what it requires,
For a mental thought, she cannot quite attain,
Being divided in two, so neither side may alter her gain,
She knows not what she wants, but is altogether self-sufficient,
She lacks a self, yet feels neither hollow nor deficient,
She wonders the streets, unaware, of who she is,
But having no impending need the world holds no allure of a quiz,
In human form, she is conscious of her instinct,
Yet in her true form, she knows not how to think,
She is deadly as a viper clad in light,
When alas she strikes, you will not have time to fight,
For her appearance is fearful, and her aura is strong,
When this siren takes her hold, you shall succumb to her sweet song,

# WATER POEMS

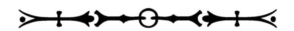

# Clarity

A clear drop running down the glass,
Moves with poise, demonstrating such class,
When it hits the sill, it makes a splash,
Its graceful decent, lacks an ending crash,
I wish I were a dew drop so simple and pure,
Its form is flawless, with an elusive allure,
Being both translucent and transparent, it lets you know all,
It has no secrets, for it has no flaw,
If I could reveal myself, as that drop of rain,
I'd have no more use for my diluted brain,
I have a cloud surrounding my soiled flesh,
It cloaks me in darkness, like an oversized dress,
I want to spin, till the cloud comes loose,
I fight its storm, yet I know its no use,
Yet if my resistance failed, would weakness overcome,
Would daylight fail, and darkness alas succumb,
I wonder why this cloud, even bothers to shield my shame,
My faults are mine, I'm the only one to blame,
I need not hide, my scars have character,
I don't have a stand in; I am my own narrator,
Sometimes I see a dew drop, as a life that could never be,
But if I were that see-through, there'd be no mystery to me.

# Wiles of Water

Wordless as a wondering brook,
Are the thoughts of a misguided crook,
He moves so quickly and plunges so deep,
A multitude of mysteries visit his sleep,
Those who fight him best beware,
For this formidable foe lacks a care,
He runs till raging, and takes till he over flows,
He's agile always and his strength ever grows,
All who try to catch him, find he slips through their fingers,
Yet even when he's gone his presence ever lingers.

# Opposites Attack

When you witness what winter can do to water,
Locked up in itself it soon grows hotter,
A ripple, a crackle, its energy at its peak,
It tickles the earth, yet the earth won't speak,
The earth takes his fill, his needs are simple,
absorbs life's nutrients till his needs are ample,
The sea so mysterious, she loves to play,
The earth heeds her call, but has little to say,
Her world is chaotic, her life a fantasy,
But the earth takes comfort in the simple sanity,
The sea, so wild, now wishes to fly,
The earth says, "leave that to the birds of the sky,"
His scoffs mean nothing, she prepares to jump,
Her waves rise high, yet fall in a slump,
The earth he chuckles till he falls on his rump,
He's got more to say, the captious chump,
"You've got no skill, you're far from strong,"
Her waters boil, and lash out in a throng,
Waves hit the earth, and then fall back in retreat,
The earth, he chuckles, "what's the matter? Can't take the heat?"
The sea burns with anger, as her tears evaporate,
She will not cry, she's filled with hate,
She knows she's strong, her stealth like a knife,
Within her waters is more than one lost life,
She's wickedly cunning, yet the earth is so laid back,
He's just so beautiful, should she really attack,
She has the ammo; the clouds are now darkening,
They're at her bidding, she can hear them barking,
The earth, he smiles, their argument forgotten,
How can he forget the fury he'd begotten?
But the rain comes gently, the rage is bottled,
She wants to fight, but her emotions are muddled,
She knows she could beat him; he hasn't half her wit,
His arrogance and pride is enough to make her sick,
She'll endure him for now she has some patience,
Her life is hot and cold it's not supposed to make sense.

# Panorama

I wake up to the scent of sweet salt air,
Then run a hand through my wind blown hair,
I rub my face then look above,
And realize I'm on a place I love,
I carefully stand knowing I had needed the rest,
As I stare down from a top the crows nest,
The crew must still sleep for the deck is clear,
The ship drifts methodically having no reason to fear,
The sky is vacant not a cloud in sight,
And I squint as I turn from the sun's great light,
The hypnotic waters smile as they catch my eye,
If I told you they didn't spark my desire, it would be a lie,
I can't help but stare as the waves kiss the ship,
They start at the bow and move to the tip,
They are so graceful their rhythm unmatched,
I watch in amazement and soon become detached,
So that I almost didn't notice when a crew member laughed,
Then calling to me asked, "My God man, are you daft?"
I shook my cumbersome thoughts and lent my mate an ear,
He chuckled once more then asked if it was clear,
I looked out yonder, and saw afar a port,
The let out a cry, "land ho!" in retort,
We were soon to be home and this trip would end,
But it wouldn't be over for the sea was now my friend,

# Water

Cold as ice, though alive with the sun,
There's no telling where the rivers dost run,
They are subtle, yet strong and stealthy,
So alive and vibrant, it's no wonder they're so healthy,
Beneath these rich waters a peace may be attained,
Surrounded by their effervescent texture, you feel a friend is gained,
Your eyes behold the glory of your surroundings,
And searching in the depths you often find things,
For they keep to their creed and hide our secrets,
But to trust the sea, always leads to regrets,
Enmeshed in water, it may seem like a game,
But the violent waters are far from tame.

# Desirable Depths

I want to be submerged beneath your cool blue depths,
I want to touch the ocean floor; I want to take those steps,
I want to see the tidal pools, be filled and then drained dry,
I want to know if underwater, it's possible to cry,
And if you can't, is it possible to be sad,
Could such a peace make you always glad?
Beneath the sea late at night, is there light like on dry land?
Could there be, despite the waters a little that dost withstand,
Though I'm sure the anemones would know their way being so alert,
Yet I can't help but wonder if I'd be that covert,
I wish that I could see the sunrise from the midst of a coral reef,
I'm sure, iridescent; the colors would be, from so far beneath,
They'd sprint and spiral as each wave went by,
As a wave washes over me my heart, begins to grieve,
Since I am void gills, I must now come up and breathe.

# INNER WORKINGS POEMS

# Heightened Sensation

I don't want to be an image; I'd prefer to be a thought,
One that sticks inside your head as though it has been caught,
As a fly caught up in a spiders web,
I make myself known as my words are read,
You cannot hear them for they come as mist,
Yet they seem so clear like the first time you kissed,
Your mind now melts as the words sink in,
Your skin starts to ripple and your breath grows thin,
These words are false, they present no facts,
But despite your efforts a fear attacks,
It sets in quickly disabling your limbs,
And alas you are subjected to all its whims,
You have no pride and you weep aloud,
You feel all alone as you push through a crowd,
You try to rationalize put up a fight,
But this fear has gained control of all but your sight,
You go where it bids, and behold untold evil,
And are gripped with a desire to hunt and to kill,
You see so much blood and your lips part to scream,
You wake up in alarm; this had all been a dream.

# Confession

I regret to inform you that this poem is a fake.
For it erupted all at once from a brain earthquake,
A ruptured thought's pulse now beats off cue,
And I struggle to remember if my lies are true,
I want to say so much all at once,
But my whims were foolish; I'm such a dunce,
To think I could have made my mark,
Yet as the light goes on, my world turns dark,
I run through wiles I fear to trace,
And chase down villains I cannot face,
I seem so strong, as I spill my guts,
Yet seek the help of others when I fall into ruts,
I'm not diseased I have no mental illness,
But when I share my thoughts there's a question to my wellness,
I talk of monsters great and strong,
And dangerous predators that don't belong,
You question my personification because you see it as truth,
When in reality to me, my whole life is a spoof,
A twisted outlook of what it is supposed to be,
You see a puddle where I see a sea,
A browning rose may seem out of place,
Yet seems so surreal locked within a glass case,
It had no power as it slowly did die,
Within its elegant tomb you almost heard it cry,
For things that seem like nothing,
Acquire the ability to be anything,
And through the words I scrawl,
They could become them all.

# Mind-Tease

I can't believe this page is empty,
When yesterday it was full,
I can't see why I see so little,
When push dost come to pull,
It's as if it has a hold on me,
One that I care not to tell,
I keep so many secrets,
Yet my words are a bottomless well,
So sour are my thoughts right now,
That it's hard for me to think,
Of what I wish to voice forth next,
Or when I'll need to drink,
The wind is on a rampage,
As it fights its way through my hair,
But then I stop to wonder,
Was the wind ever there,
Did it ever graze my skin?
Or cause this page to flip,
I should know the answer,
But I can't seem to get a grip,
Everything's so easy,
Yet I complicate it all the more,
See if I don't learn the hard way,
I can never calculate my score,
A score a fight within myself,
To see which me is better,
The one who always knows what's best,
Or the cute and carefree go-getter,
I try to defy both these two,
For neither of them can guess,
Which way I plan to turn my toes,
And who's to blame for the mess.

# Confusion at it's best

I am sick of pretending to be something I am not,
Now what was I again?
I'm lost, I've been taken, and I'm caught,
I was something else, but I can't remember when,
What was real and what was fake,
What is reality was it ever my own,
The words I knew weren't the words I spake,
My life my purpose an endless drone,
Did the words ever make sense?
They now mesh together in an endless spiel,
My life was my fantasy, it was my defense,
Its taste still lingers, it felt so real,
I'm so confused it all seems the same,
My fantasy feels like reality and vice versa,
I don't know where I went wrong but I know I'm to blame,
This is all so overwhelming but I guess it could be worse.

# Erudition

Knowledge isn't just power, its pain,
The wisdom of life is a poor excuse for gain,
You hear your brain making things clear,
Emphasizing a truth that you can't help but fear,
You want to scream as you clench your fist,
You can see your worth and you wish you didn't exist,
You are what you are no matter what you learn,
You try to act like all is well so as not to raise concern,
Washed in your faults you see how it will proceed,
To resist now is a complication you do not need.

# A Loathsome Existence

I wish that I were someone else,
But what is there I can do?
Change how I look, change who I am, if only I knew,
I could possibly consider physical alteration,
Or alter my features through augmentation,
Who would know, the change would be flawless,
The new me I create perhaps she could be faultless,
A Seer of seduction, a woman of wisdom,
My knowledge of old, would no longer be cumbersome,
I'd be someone else; my paths would hold no guile,
My mysterious face could suffer alas a smile,
My dreams are endless, I could be unknown,
Beneath my guise, I could alas suffer alone.

# FUN POEMS

# The Bell

The bell, the bell, I see the bell, swaying in the wind,
Yet not a chime will it utter,
Alone now in the opened,
It has some pride, so they say,
This is why it will not speak,
For dark are the thoughts that,
Surround this bell,
A language thou shalt not seek,
For every chime that's uttered in still,
Hast its own sound,
The music of the brave it's claimed,
It dost thunder through the ground,
Waking the molten lava,
Arousing the sleeping stones,
Disrupting the rolling mountains,
The caves then ignite their groans,
I wish that you could see it,
The Majesty of the Bell,
But for now it sways in solitude,
Within its humble shell.

# The teddy bear

I have a shanky Sharma, of very great proportion,
Yet his funny lumpy, body is void of distortion,
Sir Shanky as they call him, has a very squishy nose,
And when you turn to touch it, you feel as if he knows,
And now his giant belly, we all have come to love,
Dost bumble in quirky pattern shaking the trees above,
I love my furry friend, but is my love returned,
For to be so cute and cuddly, is a talent only earned.

# Bum on the Street

O sing for the bum,
Who drinketh the rum,
That he probably stole,
From a lad or a fool,
He has no name,
But pretends to be lame,
What a shameless game,
To be found with no name,
To live on the street,
And bask in the heat,
What a terrible way,
To spend a day,
If you were his parent,
Tell me what would you say,
I know what you'd say,
You'd say, "Wow, I'm a parent?"
And then you would say no way,
No way you can't do this,
It's dirty and wrong,
A hobo? My son?
My, what have I done?

# Cheese

Cheese as you know is yellow,
But of course at times it is grey,
But I'd advise you to eat it,
That's all I have to say,
Though there is more I wish to tell,
About the many cheeses and about the smell,
For some do smell quite awful,
Others are rather nice,
I'm not sure if I mentioned,
That cheese attracts the mice,
Not just mice but rodents of different shapes,
And sizes some are great like kangaroos,
Others are rather small,
But with a mouth full of cheese you can't help but appreciate them all.

# ROMANCE POEMS

# A Valiant End

Beneath the trees of a meadow fair,
There lay a maiden, with a lustrous hair,
To her face, there was no light,
The once bright earth no lay in night,
The crystal streams, they now run red,
Deprived of mirth, for all is dead,
Her last words spoken, brought upon such doom,
Chivalrous valour hath weaved her tomb.

# The Angel

Along a quiet rippling brook,
There slept an angel whom all forsook,
He had needed time; he had needed to be bold,
But fury is weak in contrast to his heart of gold,
For though this knave was strong, and bright,
The slightest fall hath dimmed his light,
His patience gone, his energy spent,
For once in his life, mortal words hath left a dent,
A hole, a blow of emotional proportion,
An open stab wound, that flows like the ocean,
For words can hurt like nothing else,
They bring great pain to those with stealth,
The angel wakes, his lashes flutter,
He rumples his hair, his lips do mutter,
His thoughts are muddled; his stance is far from sober,
Drunk with self loathing, he feels his life is over,
Although immortal beauty surrounds his flesh,
He desires only that his and mortal may mesh,
Love with hate, desire with dread,
A young man's cliché, colors the cheeks in red,
Rejected once, humbled twice,
By a simple beauty, with words like ice,
To ask again, would be ill-advised,
But low that angel saw his future in her eyes,
Skin-like bronze, hair an iridescent gold,
The sun hath shown her its favor, and without her, it is cold,
He won't give up, he knows that now,
His heart, relentless, shall strengthen his vow,
His cocky spirit, all at once contrite,
He had been a fool, but he will make things right.

# A fearful gaze

Your eyes, the sunrise no color, its gray,
For it's your eyes that now bring forth the day,
I light dost shine within them, like unto the moon,
The mere sight of which could make a strong man swoon,
A sea, so vast is embellished within those eyes,
I swear the likes of which could out shine the skies,
Your eyes like gem stones, they glitter and glow,
They penetrate deep I fear what they know.

# Victory in Weakness

I never thought I'd have the heart to tell you how I felt,
When I chocked down your lines, I admit my heart did melt,
I could not shake you, you had a hold. The question was on what,
You were so sweet and kind, yet your walk was never short of a strut,
You liked your life and you liked me in it,
But the aftertaste always made me spit,
You were so fake; your skin was surely plether,
Yet I took the bait, and relinquished my empty tether,
I was unarmed my defenses leveled,
I let you in though my mind rebelled,
My senses had always been well tuned,
Yet they'd failed to catch me when I swooned,
I cannot have this; I will not be won,
If I sank any deeper, I knew I would succumb,
I took hold my heart and slaughtered its essence,
I no longer wished to endure, its stale presence,
It cut me deep though, I knew I'd survived worse,
When another blow hit me, I uttered a curse,
The blow had stung for just a second,
Yet if I didn't act fast the wound would never mend,
I turned alas to face my foe and the villain extended a hand,
I knew to accept would cripple me under the weight of his command,
I sneered at the act and stood my ground, ignoring the lingering pain,
My foe did watch my every move unsure if I was sane,
I could not cry though my eyes felt the heat,
If I could not hold my own, I'd have to accept defeat,
He caught my gaze and moved in my direction,
Then my limbs turned stiff, as I stared at my reflection,
It was not me, I would not allow it, and I knew I'd gone too far,
He released my sight and loosed his hold, yet I knew he'd set the bar,
He had struck first, though I had not been prepared,
For the crippling truth that alas he still cared,
He was always there and always would be the face of what could have been,
Yet I cared little and it gave me power so I knew in the end I'd win,
He had been a rival, a vicious threat, a caring friend,
I had confessed I loved him; it was a curse I had to end,
I brought forth spite, I showed no emotion,
When I denied what was sacred, I might has well have been the ocean,
For my words had consumed him as I knew they would,
I had won the battle yet knew not what was good,
For I'd lost all feeling and my heart was numb,
He had been my victory, how could I be so dumb.

# Divine Destiny

In my errand I found a light
Fate hath brought me here tonight,
Immersed in radiance, I sought to fight,
To slay the darkness, that haunts the night,
Alas kismet found me amidst the fright,
To tend my wounds, for I was smite,
Her gentle words hath cleared my sight,
And lulled me from my mindless plight,
My destiny attained, yet not in might,
Amidst terror, it found me, however contrite,
For it came to my aid, as a maiden in white,

# Blind-sighted

By and by there was a knight,
Strong with valour and great with might,
He was not one to start a fight,
Yet nobility, brought on, a greater plight,
For by sorcery hath he abandoned light?
A vixen fair hath blinded his sight,

# A Restless Heart

Behold afar there was a knave,
Young at heart, yet strong and brave,
His valiant deeds, were known abroad,
His skill with the blade, by his own hands sod,
Contrite, however was this lad,
Yet rarely did one see him sad,
For scarcely had he friendless been,
Being rich with such pleasantries, not often seen,
Free spirit, was his creed, in truth,
A child, set apart at youth,
For though his deeds were great and noble,
Deep down inside, his heart was woeful,
For never before, had he felt the sting,
Of cupid's arrow, that makes the heart sing,
But longing's taste was O so bitter,
So His duty's expanded as he grew fitter,
Work and merriment became his guise,
Until an old friend, bewitched his fair eyes,
The years had changed, both their sight,
Their immature youth, now a beacon of light,
For in their childhood a bond was made,
Their longing quenched, whilst hearts were swayed.

# Strangled Bond

Why, when I try to take a chance,
Do you hold me fast and stay my advance,
You tell me no, while your eyes scream yes,
You silence my words, when I go to confess,
I thought this was what you asked for,
To stay this way forever is there something more,
I wished, I screamed, I said a prayer,
You said you loved, I know, I was there,
When you took my hand, you were so gentle,
You held my gaze and touched my temple,
Your touch, it reached inside my soul,
So I took a hint, I'm such a fool,
Tell me this was all a dream,
Convince my heart to change its theme,
Force my brain to think once more,
Do it now and even the score,
I am not weak; you made me this way,
You made me need you; it's needless to say,
I don't regret it, I made my choice,
My strength is yours, for you gave me my voice
And to the depths of my soul you gave light
You made my heart alive; you did it out of spite,
So what is it, you say, was your intent,
For your actions were always pure and gallant,
You never strayed, when I grew restless,
You were my shield, when I felt defenseless,
You never lied; your words were truth,
I was the mystery, you were my sleuth.

# The Surrender

You're not that clever, you couldn't be,
Your thoughts are unguarded, they're wild and free,
So tell me how you did it, I beg you I must know,
How can someone so simple, overnight become a pro,
When you spoke the words were foreign, for they could not be your own,
Your expression was strange to me, like something I'd never known,
I had you figured your actions clocked,
I had told you its over; I presumed you had walked,
But you asked me a question, deceptive yet smart,
And with my mind no longer guarded, I surrendered to you my heart.

# Writing Wrongs

How dare my mind betray me this way,
It did not let me think of what to say,
How careless can my feeble mind be?
When my senses are blurred, so I cannot see,
Let it die, let the feelings go,
But the more I say it, the more they grow,
I tried to hide my heart from pain,
Yet you searched unsullied against the grain,
It hadn't been offered there was no fee,
Yet somehow you produced a key,
A key I barely dreamed existed,
You claimed a place while my thoughts were misted,
And even when I took a stand,
You did not waver at my command,
Instead you stood still, till it drove me nuts,
And the next move you made, proved you had guts,
I'd driven my point but alas was weak,
When the silence ended, no longer did I speak,
Our questions had been answered though not a word was said,
For in that one brief moment, both our hearts were fed.

# Love

When love comes down, it spreads its wing,
It blinds your sight but you don't feel a thing,
It colors your world in shades of light,
The summer sun rises to end a fluorescent night,
You feel alive like never before,
Your world is chaos but never a chore,
You want to sing though your lungs are frail,
With that one special phrase your face grows pale,
But you're not afraid, all fear is dead,
For life itself is a figment in your head,
It's so unreal nothing seems right,
Life's endless beauty an overwhelming delight,
For in that split second when love shows its face,
You are fully submerged in fantastical grace.

# The Successor

Blinded by darkness, you fought your way through,
You brushed back the rigid branches, where they inconveniently grew,
It was not like you to fall, though you stumbled once or twice,
You were not likely to fail, but your confidence had a price,
An unseen nemesis let his claws take hold,
A devastating blow that did humble the bold,
You ripped from its grasp searing your tender flesh,
Then fell to the ground causing blood and earth to mesh,
The wound it burned as you knew it would,
But you ignored the pain and cut through the wood,
The blow was strong despite your wounded muscle,
And the deadly forest fell amidst the fiery tussle,
It would not overcome you; you could not accept defeat,
But as the forest walls gave way, you sought all at once to retreat,
That which you saw would easily make a weaker man grow faint,
For the beast that stood before you now, was anything but quaint,
It arose high above you, eclipsing the sun,
If you had remembered how to move you were sure you would've run,
When your senses returned you stood your ground it was unlikely you were sane,
But you grit your teeth and abandoned your fear till the beast alas was slain,
How you did it I'll never know but you destroyed my present threat,
You brought me down from a tower high and you did it without regret.

# Counterproductive

The stunts I often pull are very far from reckless,
And though I'm never there, I wouldn't say I'm feckless,
I have a life I have goals that are quite feasible,
And when we argue over our present life I'd say I'm pretty reasonable,
You're brave, you're bold, and your words remain undaunted,
So tell me why even when your home, your house, appears so haunted,
You seem so distant even when we're close,
Your gentle touch is like that of a ghost,
My muscles tense as I prep for a shudder,
Your sycophantic words fade to nothing more than a mutter,
Apprehension overtakes me as our fight dies down,
As the ferment passes it takes with it your frown,
I feel it's over all anguish is gone,
Your eyes appraise me, as your smile begins to fawn,
I've missed that smile; it'd been long since I'd last seen it,
It forgave my incompetence, but could you possible mean it,
I knew you did as your words turned timid,
Dare I ask just yet if magic was admitted?
If it were I care not to know,
Since a radiant motion all at once did glow.

# Immunization

There is a verse in Genesis two,
That speaks of an innocence I never knew,
That one sweet innocence that could change my perspective,
Did all at once become an elective,
Stripped of our sanctity our desires grow evil,
This makes us all too vulnerable towards our precarious seal,
The seal that binds our love together,
Now so easily is discarded for another,
I know not why, but in truth it's very simple,
Our minds now so vile, soon forget we are a temple,
This world is pathetic and mates aren't scarce,
That sacred bonding promise is nothing but a farce,
I want nothing of it, I wouldn't survive,
I could not jump and fall and still be alive,
My heart is weak and my need is great,
Should I back out now or accept my fate?

# Calculated Courtship

It's strange to think that when we spoke all we did was disagree,
And even though we've only just met, I feel as if he knows me,
When he asks me questions I can't help but comply,
He always finds my weakness yet I can't understand why,
Why when he looks, he can see the true me,
His obvious smarts could calculate my destiny,
He is so perfect He couldn't possibly be real,
Yet when I let him read my work he knows just how I feel,
Trapped within a world where we're a slave to the unknown,
And even while we're among friends, we still feel all alone,
We feel so trapped in this world our cage,
And yet we still wish that we did not age,
For if we lived forever maybe then we'd find the truth,
And we'd know then if the world could ever be found by a sleuth,
We ponder these thoughts and perhaps look them up,
We then finish our search but we have not given up,
We stare at one another till our laughs break the silence,
We know we are too different and yet there's other evidence.

# Fantasy

Wake up princess it's not what it seems,
This real life world is all in your dreams,
You sleep so long and see so much,
Yet all you need to awake, is but a single touch,
You live in a world that is all a ruse,
You put up a guard for fear one might abuse,
It's not your life yet you hide in this insanity,
Where the purity of love is turned to vile vanity,
You work so hard for the things you love,
When you need but to ask to receive all the above,
My love is strong and will never fail,
I slew every dragon that was ever on your tail,
Why do you deny me your presence when you sleep?
I tell you all yet secrets you still keep,
Look at me my love don't let this tower become your tomb,
Abandon all your heedless worries and come up from the gloom,
I will not let you go you already seem so pale,
Wake up and embrace that your life is a fairy tale.

# My Angel

When I saw your face I couldn't believe what I was seeing,
A picture of perfection a celestial being,
Your eyes were livid as a golden sunset,
Your presence was daunting each time we met,
You seemed so impenetrable like that of cherubim,
Your confidence matchless like unto seraphim,
You appeared so angelic while surrounded in light,
Yet were dark and mysterious as an angel of night,
I felt so powerless while in your presence,
Yet despite it all I retained my confidence,
A whisper is heard through all the tranquility,
I alas found peace amidst my humility.

# Inconsistently Constant

Why, When I try to take a chance,
Do you hold me fast and stay my advance?
You tell me no, while your eyes scream yes,
You silence my words, when I go to confess,
I thought this what you asked for,
To stay this way forever, is there something more?
I wished, I screamed, I said a prayer,
You said you loved me, I know, I was there,
When you took my hand, you were so gentle,
You held my gaze and touched my temple,
Your touch it reached inside my soul,
So I took a hint, I'm such a fool,
Tell me this was all a dream,
Convince my heart to change its theme,
Force my brain to think once more,
Do it now and even the score,
I am not weak; you made me this way,
You made me need you; it's needless to say,
I don't regret it, I made my choice,
My strength is yours, for you gave me my voice,
And to the depths of my soul you gave light,
You made my heart alive; you did it out of spite,
So what is it, you say, was your intent?
For your actions were always pure and gallant,
You never strayed, when I grew restless,
You were my shield, when I felt defenseless,
You never lied; your words were truth,
I was the mystery, you were my sleuth,

# The Dagmar

Colored in gray, the shades grew bright,
Her brush with death hath altered her sight,
For darkness is brilliant, while daylight is dull,
Relentless hope, will keep her soul full,
Long will she wait?
To rekindle the flame, that brought her fate,
For natures alas has gone too far,
When it cursed the race that is Dagmar,
Deprived of feeling, they seek out pain,
One man's mortality, for another man's gain,
Yet he a Halfling differed from the rest,
Despite his bloodlust this creature was blessed,
For deep in his soul their dwelt some emotion,
Of this he prized and turned to devotion,
To which he gave to her, his foe,
This small price he paid, to ease his woe,
For while the wars raged hot and fierce,
These enemies' hearts, cupid's arrow alas did pierce.

# The Race

We made are way down a lonely road,
Hand in hand, alone we strode,
Sometimes I wished that you were here,
I felt your presence you were so near,
If I could see you I think I'd feel better,
If I knew the words, I'd write you a letter,
You seem so close when you're far away,
The sight of your name seems to brighten my day,
The road stretches on but your hands are clenched,
An action brought on by something vital being wrenched,
You know not why but you feel something is missing,
I hear the wind, sweeping through me like its hissing,
I look to my left and see nothing but darkness,
I reach to my right and feel a tree branch gently caress,
The loneliness subsides as the forest comes alive,
As terror sets in my thoughts are only will I survive,
You let out a sigh but on my side it's a scream,
I turn to defend but it decays like in a dream,
I feel your presence; I hear your voice,
I cry out loud, the sound is an unintelligible noise,
The path slopes down, the ground is thick,
I begin to sink my feet they stick,
I can not move, the woods begin to howl,
Anger wells within and I let out a growl,
Someone watches, from a top a hill,
Their stance is tense, they aim to kill,
I shrink to the earth, and try to claw my way free,
The action is futile; they've already seen me,
The predator advances, and chuckles at my predicament,
I look for help but see only a darkened firmament,
Something tears my flesh; a scream is quelled in pain,
I flail my arms and try to fight the movement is in vain,
I have to fight my leg alas comes free,
I kick, they choke, but not because of me,
A tussle begins, but my limbs feel frail and useless,
A cry is uttered, I'd defend but I'm defenceless,
I'm covered in blood; a movement to stand takes all my might,
My saviour he sees and is prompted to end the fight,
A single blow drives the beast to the earth,
A bottled anger displayed for all its worth,

The Fight was won, yet hadn't been planned,
My body collapses; I haven't the strength to stand,
A familiar hand catches me and lowers me to the ground,
You free my other foot, and make sure I'm safe and sound,
I did not see you on the path; you were never really there,
You smiled in the darkness, and touched my curly hair,
I'm caught off guard by your sudden case capricious,
I try to be frank, but mellowness has never suited us,
I shove you away, but the action is nothing short of pathetic,
You dramatically fact your hurt, you've always been more athletic,
I don't want to continue, I want to melt into your embrace,
But you lift me from the ground, you no longer wish to race,

# BATTLE POEMS

# The War

Remember my name, for it's the last thing you'll hear,
I tense and remember the end is near,
The battle at its peak and the war wages fierce and strong,
Yet I fear my time is up, yet the waiting seems so long,
I've done my part; I've given my all,
The wounds I've received are very far from small,
I'd cry out for help if it would do any good,
Many great have fallen it's a miracle I've withstood,
I feel great pain yet at the same time am numb,
I'm poised with my defiance I probably look so dumb,
I am but nothing save an able bodied soul,
I've taken quite a beating yet for that I am a fool,
I never should have come for the death I face is grim,
I turn to block an advance and save a wounded limb,
I'm nothing short of weary yet my body moves as directed,
I slay another foe, yet feel a dagger injected,
The blade doesn't twist for the hand goes limp,
The knave who planted it was nothing more than a wimp,
An adrenaline pulses as the blood starts to flow,
And I jump into action overcoming each foe,
In my side the dagger remains as a reminder to myself,
That the mistakes I have made only added to my stealth,
The battle alas raged hot, and I could feel the end draw nigh,
When I saw that we had won I felt as if I could never die,
I dropped my weapon and collapsed to the ground,
Alas amidst such turmoil, such a peace was found.

# Why me?

Waiting, wondering, will it ever be my way,
Shall it in time find me, or will I fade away,
Will I ever be noticed, will the sun lend a ray,
When I open my heart, will that be the day,
Or will the tears fall, and the sky turn gray,
When I pour out my soul, what will they say?
Will the ocean roar? Will I feel its spray?
The message is clear, that day is today,
I do not fear, my spirit, it will not slay,
For my mind is strong, my courage doth not fray,
I am ready to speak, I shall no longer delay.

# A Friend who Sticks

Black like darkness I stood alone,
White like snow the cold made me groan,
Blue like water I had a need,
For red like blood my hands did bleed,
Brown like earth, to which my body fell,
Green like mold now pollutes my sense of smell,
Yellow like sunshine, my skin was warmed,
Green like herbs healed all that was deformed,
Brown like chocolate the air was sweet,
For red like rubies the setting sun shone elite,
Blue like birds a song took flight,
White like stars I saw a bright light,
Black like darkness I'm not alone.

# An Oxymoron's Truth

When the wild pacifist, flees to stay,
Searches in earnest, while asleep in the hay,
He eats to starve, and drinks till parched,
With eyes wide shut, all things were watched,
He sits to stand, forgets to recall,
While he chats with the mute and short men stand tall,
A virgin vodka, dost sober his drunkenness,
Absinthe sweetens, while honey is bitterness,
Lulled by adrenaline, he wakes to sleep,
Boisterous now, he does not make a peep,
He loves what he hates, yet hates love itself,
His greed is petty, yet he's poor with wealth.

# Peace

Peace, I ask you, is there such a thing,
What ramifications could this simple word bring?
Would I bring forth turmoil as most things did?
Could it strip you of your ground, and cause your feet to skid,
Your answer is no, but how can I believe,
That this word in its essence could heal me as I grieve,
I knew not peace it had never existed, at least so I thought,
How could this marvelous verb in truth, be all that I had sought,
My fears were vivid they had taken a form,
But amidst my new discovery, my thoughts alas were warm,
I sank within this strange new emotion,
That to me, for some reason held devotion,
It was not real I had to be dreaming,
My once frozen heart was now alas steaming,
I had never felt this it had never been my own,
But amidst my marred exterior this feeling of peace found a home.

# Lasting Life

Believe what you will but I speak the truth,
Though I know you have trouble taking advice from a youth,
Believe me I've changed I am not who you knew,
For amidst this great adversity I somehow grew,
I once knew fear like it were my brother,
But since that fateful day it no longer is my cover,
I now run free unafraid of my shadow,
Fear no longer knows my name; it was swallowed in my woe,
Though I do not wish to go there all that is in the past,
I dwell now in a joy of untold sweetness, which I know shall forever last.

# Whole Armor

Subtlety is a sultry thing and very easily weasels its way in,
Its attack is gradual as it turns you to sin,
This subtlety it is a tool of the devil.
He works at your defenses, making them level,
His wiles are a wondrous thing to behold,
He keeps us guessing as his plot dost unfold,
We have a great armor yet we turn to wrong,
Since we often forget to put it on,
We feel we're strong and can stand against our foes,
But without God close, we fall by their arrows,
In the evil day the fight will come so great,
But if you're not prepared it will be thus too late,
Your weakness will be found and your defenses then deployed,
Without God's heavenly armor you will alas be destroyed.

# Night Drive

As I make my down a haunted highway,
Shadows stare as if to say,
"I've got you now you're going to fall",
"You're going to crash and lose it all",
"You have no hope; I'm in your view",
"When we collide, it's the end of you",
"I've watched you closely, you're carefree and reckless",
"You never expected, I'd be this feckless",
"You believed I'd hide and remain a shadow",
"You thought if you ignored me perhaps I'd go",
"I'm in your face, yet it seems like slow motion",
"Now how do you avoid a wave of the ocean?",
Metal to flesh having flesh like metal,
Our embrace is a drive-by, I will not settle,
You don't scare me, yet my mouth remains ajar,
You left a dent a visible scar,
I mend the wound, yet the memory remains
All I can think is, "why didn't I change lanes,"
You've made your point and next time I'll beware,
I'll mind that subtle sign that warns "handle with care".

# A peace in parting

Through a winter so cold,
I fought its fiery chill,
I slew the icy roads,
Its black ice sank in heaps,
I will not know the end,
Not till I say my peace,
For in this worlds darkest winter,
A mighty foe arose,
His strength was as the melting sea,
No one would dare appose,
Yet I a mere child,
High on summer's breeze,
Feared not of my own end,
Yet that of the deciduous tree's,
A life of peril,
All at once lay ahead,
A war did wage at winters peak,
It was a fight to raise the dead,
This lifeless world I swear will live again,
The sun dost hide, yet it need not fear,
For its presence fills my heart with cheer,
Its light will aid me, if it dares come out
"These clouds are weak! You need not doubt!"
The sun it hears my cry,
And all at once it fills the sky,
It dries my tears as the spring flowers bloom,
This world once more is void of gloom,

# Where Fear and Death part Ways

Broken beneath the surface, crushed amidst my disease,
I wander in a desert place; my mind is ill at ease,
The nights, their terror, I now must face, my foes they come in threes,
Their voices, taunt, a menacing bass, I turn to run, yet fall to my knees,
The sun, now gone, lets darkness flow at will,
My tyrants, vast, now move in for the kill,
Death, it lingers, an icy, chilling torment,
It's taste a burning flame in which I writhe, and rant,
I flail, I falter, I cry in vanity,
I shriek, I shudder, I've lost my sanity,
This can't be death, there's too much pain,
I look to the heavens, and am showered in rain,
The sun comes out, a rainbow shines in radiance,
I've never been more peaceful, in all my existence.

# LIFE POEMS

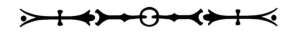

# Betrayal

You fed me your farce, strangled our bond in lies,
Now my pity, as it were, is not shaken by your cries,
I mean nothing to you, our friendship means nothing
I think as I sit, for if it did mean something your car would be where I left it,
I see how this has all been a joke, as you sit in his presence enveloped in his smoke,
You'd rather spend your time with the guy, who is using you,
Than the girl who cares for you,
Can't you see it is all a ruse? for until you do yourself in entirety he will surely use,
You're not only hurting yourself you know, you're hurting me,
See if anything happens to you I'll blame myself ,
For ever believing you were capable of taking on my trust,
It's me your hurting because it's me who hurt you by giving you your keys.

# Girls are Stupid!

Plain as power, simple as submission,
To quench one's hearts thirst, has become an obsession,
You seek out aid, yet accept no help,
Being carefree and careless you've become such a whelp,
You have fallen so often, and your errs have taken a toll,
It's as if you're on your way home, then suddenly hit a pole,
You are so stupid your antics a joke,
You assume your folly will land you a bloke,
I warn you you'll get hurt, and his depth is a gimmick,
You tell me I'm the stupid one, and then call me a cynic,
You could be right, since I've never strayed too far,
But the truth is I'd take pride over some deadbeat with a car,
I suppress a smile as you tell me I'm wrong,
Then dismiss the conversation since your rants are always long,
I take my leave since as you know I hate this fight,
I'll be prepping my "I told you so" till at least tomorrow night.

# Contented wanting

Even though I have so much, I feel indifferent when people complain,
Is it because my conscious is so great or am I the one that's vain,
I strive to look my best, yet am compelled to jump in mud,
Is this animal instinct, like the cow who chews the cud?
It may be a misconception, since I'm very far from wise,
But the airs I put on while I'm in public are nothing but a guise,
A guise I wear O so well, while surrounded by an audience,
I think I'm still there but when I look there is no pending evidence,
I'm all but lost behind my façade, though no one could ever tell,
Since this mask fits so perfectly, on my face it shall dwell,
Beneath this mask, I feel so clever my fear is all but gone,
Without it on I feel exposed like something might go wrong,
I need to be rid of this I need to come out and be me,
I feel my chains; they have to go I need to be set free,
If someone were to break my chains could I then get up and go?
I know I want this I can almost taste it and yet I'm thinking no.

# TREE POEMS

# The Root

With great fear thou shalt know hope's grace,
For hope comes from faith, not seeing face to face,
Fear comes from evil one believes will never die,
Let love be your shield from all that dost draw nigh,
Transformed in your faith you have no need of fear,
Even in the ending times you know new life is near,

# The Tree

You ask me why I dress in black,
I tell you "It's not coming back,
You ask me 'what' and why "blue and red?"
I tell you in sorrow my tree is dead,
The red and blue are the blood and sweat,
He never failed me I owe him a debt,
I swung from his limbs without a care,
When I lost my footing, he was always there,
He had a branch for every mood,
When he cradled me close a melody ensued,
His branches enticed me, with them, I did dance,
When they dipped me back I was in a trance,
The world it spun but we stood still,
It slowly faded, it was not my will,
Fungus took hold and choked his slender frame,
He slowly weakens; I'm the one to blame,
It was too much, my touch is poison,
With the sun MIA, it can only worsen,
Take my hand, take my all,
Unravel your cradle, and let me fall,
You left my side, at your side I will leave,
To your hollow trunk forever, I will cleave.

# The Songbird's Tree

High above a great old tree,
There dwelt a songbird, young and free,
Yet ever did this young bird lust,
After such a lovely tree, whom it held such trust,
The tree hugged the earth, like as it were its child,
Brushed away the wind, when it sought to defile,
The fruit of this tree, it ever did nurture,
Holding fast their stems, till their season of departure,
O how I wish I were great thought the bird to itself,
To be rooted with valour, and mighty with stealth,
To forever be strong, my years never wasted,
A guardian always, a mighty mother to all created,
The tree held a home for the bird as it desired,
Till curiosity got the best of the tree, and it inquired,
"Why stay you" asked the tree to the bird,
"When your wings are strong and your voice not yet heard,"
"It's because I love thee" the songbird answered,
And am astounded by your majesty, though abased and never heard,
The great tree chuckled, a hearty laugh,
This startled the bird, thinking he must be daft,
The bird cried out "Why dost my envy stir such laughter,"
The tree answered back, "Because it is your life that I hath hungered after,"
"You so free so full of youth and yet so eager to waste your life,"
"To cling forever to me through all my strife,"
"Though in my heart your love, I do return,"
"And yet also I hold friendship, which is the reason for concern,"
"I love thee dear and do wish thee much,"
"But amidst my branches thou shalt find none such,"
"For you were born to roam the earth,"
"Spread your beauty and share your mirth,"
"Now you wish for majesty, and to be great,"
"Well the heavens are beckoning, join them, therein lay's your fate".

Despite what everyone says their are no limits to my future and I don't plan on shooting for anything less then what I ultimately am able to achieve.

-Celestial Siren